Weekly Reader Books presents

What to do when your mom or dad says "CLEAN YOURSELF UP!"

By
JOY WILT BERRY

Living Skills Press
Fallbrook, California

Distributed by:

Word, Incorporated
4800 W. Waco Drive
Waco, TX 76703

CREDITS

Producer
  Ron Berry

Editor
  Orly Kelly

Weekly Reader Books edition published by
arrangement with Living Skills Press.

Dear Parents:

"CLEAN YOURSELF UP!" You've probably said that more than once to your child and received a less than enthusiastic response. Has it ever occurred to you that your child's resistance to your request may come from not knowing **how** to do what you have asked? The assumption that a child will automatically know how to fulfill a request is often the cause of much parent-child conflict.

If you expect your children to do something they are not equipped to do, it is most likely that they will become overwhelmed and anxious while you become frustrated. Both reactions are prime conditions for an argument!

Why not avoid these kinds of encounters? Who needs them? Much of the negative "back and forth" which goes on between you and your child can be avoided if both of you approach your expectations intelligently.

Fulfilling **any** expectation always begins with knowing how. Skills are required to do any task, no matter what the task may be. These skills must be learned **before** the task can be accomplished. This is a fact of life!

All too often parents have left their children to discover these skills on their own through trial and error over a very long period of time. But why should this be so? You wouldn't give your child a complicated book in the beginning and say, "Teach yourself to read!"

My suspicion is that most parents take certain skills so much for granted, they forget that these skills must be taught.

Does this apply to you? If it does, **relax** because **"CLEAN YOURSELF UP!"** not only helps children, it helps parents survive as well.

If you will take the time to go through this book with your child, both of you will learn some valuable skills ... skills that will really pay off in the long run.

Some children will be able to read the book and assimilate all of the information themselves; however, in most cases you'll get better, longer lasting results if you use the "show me how, then let me do it" method. Here's how it works:

Using this book as a guideline ...
1. Demonstrate how the task should be done by doing it yourself while your child watches.
2. Do the task together or encourage your child to do the task while you watch. (Avoid criticizing his or her efforts, and praise anything done correctly while you are watching.)
3. Let your child do the task alone.
4. Praise your child's work and express appreciation for what he or she has done.

If you'll take a little bit of time to teach your children the skills they need to fulfill your requests, you'll save yourself a lot of energy in the long haul.

So don't just sit there – do it, and have fun while you're at it. Who knows, doing these nitty-gritty things with your child may give you some of the greatest experiences you'll ever have together, and surely some of the most rewarding.

Sincerely,

Joy Wilt Berry

Has your mother or father told you to ...

CLEAN YOURSELF UP!

Whenever your mom or dad tells you to clean yourself up, do you wonder ...

If any of this sounds familiar to you, you're going to **love** this book!

Because it will tell you exactly how to clean yourself up and keep yourself that way.

HOW TO CLEAN YOUR HAIR

Try to shampoo and rinse your hair every day. If you can't do it every day, you should do it at least three days a week. You can do this as part of your daily shower, or you can do it in a sink.

9

Step 1

Brush your hair for a few
minutes to remove
any loose dirt and tangles.

Step 2

Get your hair and scalp
completely wet.

SHAMPOOING

Step 3

Put about one or two teaspoons of shampoo into your hand and work gently into your hair
and work up a lather. (Some shampoos are
concentrated, so you should use a smaller
amount of them.) Using your fingertips,
massage the shampoo into your scalp and work
it out to the ends of the hair.

Step 4

Leave the shampoo on your hair for about two
minutes. If your hair is very dirty, you might
want to rinse out the shampoo and repeat steps
3 and 4 before you move on.

RINSING

Step 5

Rinse all the shampoo out of your hair.

Step 6

Put approximately one tablespoon of cream
rinse into your hand and work into your hair.
Use your fingertips to massage it into your
scalp and out to the ends of your hair.

Step 7

Leave the cream rinse on your hair for about two minutes.

Step 8

Rinse all the cream rinse out of your hair.

THE SQUEAK TEST

It's important to get all the shampoo and rinse out of your hair because, if any is left in, it can make your hair look dull and dirty. To make sure all the shampoo and rinse are out of your hair, give it the "squeak test" by sliding your hand over your hair. If it squeaks, it's clean. If your hand glides, you still have soap or rinse in your hair.

Step 9

Dry your hair as well as possible with a clean, dry towel.

Step 10

Comb your hair with a clean comb, and style it the way you want it to be when it is dry. To clean your comb or brush, fill the sink or a bowl with warm water and add a tablespoon of sudsy ammonia. Leave your brush and comb in this mixture for about 15 minutes. At the end of this time rub the brush and comb together to scrub them both thoroughly. If your brush has natural bristles, do not use ammonia but a small amount of soap and warm water for the cleaning mixture.

Choose a hair style which fits your face and is easy for you to take care of by yourself. Your hair style should let your hair go its natural way.

CONDITIONING YOUR HAIR

You should condition your hair at least twice a month, to make it shinier, softer and better looking.

To condition your hair, complete steps 1 - 8 and then massage approximately one table-spoon of conditioner into your scalp and out to the ends of your hair.

Leave the conditioner on for about five minutes and then rinse it completely out of your hair.

To take extra good care of your hair ...

Avoid:

brushing your hair when it is wet, because wet hair breaks easily;

using hair blowers, curling wands, and electric rollers, because too much heat can damage your hair.

Avoid:

putting curlers in your hair carelessly, or sleeping on them, because this can damage your hair;

going to bed with a wet head, because your hair will dry in all sorts of funny, unmanageable ways.

CLEANING YOUR EYES

It is important to clean around your eyes every day, preferably in the morning. Use a clean, damp washcloth to wash the area all around your eyes. Be sure to get into the corners and gently clean out any dirt that may have collected there.

Avoid putting anything other than water on the washcloth, because soap and other chemicals can irritate your eyes.

CLEANING YOUR EARS

It is important to clean your ears every day. Put a clean, damp washcloth over your index finger and wash in and around each ear. Make sure you wash behind your ears and get inside all the cracks and folds.

Avoid putting anything in your ear other than a washcloth, because anything smaller might get lodged inside your ear and could damage it.

CLEANING YOUR NOSE

It is important to clean your nose every day.
Blow your nose to remove any loose dirt that
may have collected there.

Put a clean, damp washcloth over your index
finger and wash the inside of your nose.

If you don't have a clean, damp washcloth and there is something inside your nose, use a handkerchief or tissue instead.

Avoid cleaning your nose without a washcloth, handkerchief, or tissue draped over your finger.

CLEANING YOUR MOUTH

It is important to brush your teeth at least twice a day and to floss them at least once a day.

Step 1
Wet your toothbrush. You should use the kind that has soft bristles and rounded tips.

Step 2
Put about one-half inch of fluoride toothpaste on the wet toothbrush.

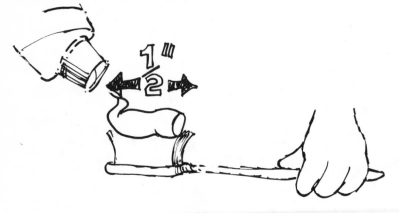

Step 3

Using small rounded scrubbing motions and working from the back to the front of your mouth, brush the fronts of your teeth.

Step 4

Using the same motions, brush the backs of your teeth and then the tops.

Be sure to brush your gums gently as well as your teeth.

Step 5

Rinse out your mouth with water.

Step 6

Get about eighteen inches of dental floss and wrap the ends around your index fingers. Use your thumbs to hold the dental floss firmly in position if you need to.

Step 7

Work the floss gently between two of your teeth.

Step 8

Rub the floss up and down the side of one tooth and then the other.

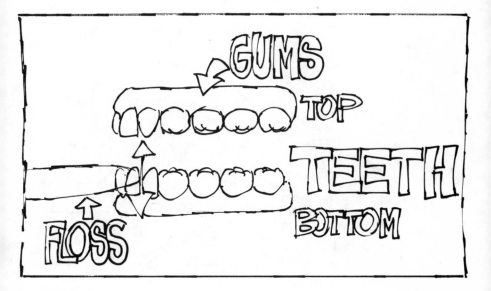

Step 9

Working from the back to the front of your mouth, floss between all your teeth.

Step 10

Rinse out your mouth with water. You may want to add some mouthwash to the water you use for your final rinse.

Avoid using a worn-out toothbrush. If your toothbrush is old and worn out, throw it away and get a new one.

CLEANING YOUR FACE

It is important to clean your face at least twice a day. One of the times can be while you are taking your daily bath or shower.

To clean your face:

Step 1

Make a lather in your hands with the soap. Use a mild facial soap, not a deodorant soap.

Step 2

Using small circular motions, gently apply the lather to your face with your fingertips.

Step 3

Rinse the lather off your face by splashing clean warm water on it.

After you have rinsed your face with warm water, you might want to freshen it by splashing cold water on it.

Step 4

Blot your face dry with a clean dry towel. Don't rub your face with the towel.

After your face is dry, you might want to put face cream or lotion on it. To do this:

Step 1

Put a dot of the cream or lotion on your forehead, nose, chin, and cheeks.

Step 2

Gently work it into your skin with your fingertips, using single strokes that begin toward the center of the face and work out. Do not rub your face or pull your skin.

CLEANING YOUR BODY

It is important to take a shower or bath every day. If you usually shower, you might want to take a bath once a week to soak off ground-in dirt.

Plain water and a clean washcloth are enough to clean most of your body, but you should use a deodorant soap

> under your arms,
>
> between your legs (in the buttocks and genital area),
>
> on your hands (especially between your fingers and under your nails), and
>
> on your feet (especially between your toes and under your toenails).

Use a small brush each time you take a shower or bath to clean between your fingers and toes and under your nails. Also use the brush on your elbows and on and around your heels.

Older girls who have developed breasts should use soap around and under their breasts.

PROTECTING YOUR SKIN

After your shower or bath, you may want to put on body lotion. Lotion helps to replace the moisture that is lost from too much sun and polluted air, so put it on any area of your body that won't be covered by clothing.

If you decide to put lotion on, be sure to put an extra amount on your hands, elbows, and heels.

SMELLING GOOD

If you plan to be around other people, you may want to use an underarm deodorant. Underarm deodorant is usually put on in the morning after a shower or bath.

For an extra special smell, girls might want to put perfume or cologne behind their ears and on their wrists.

Boys might want to put men's cologne or aftershave lotion on their faces and necks.

CLEANING YOUR HANDS AND FEET

Give yourself a manicure (treatment for the hands) and a pedicure (treatment for the feet) once a week. If you can't do it once a week, you should do it at least once or twice a month.

Step 1

Trim your nails carefully with a pair of cuticle scissors or a nail clipper. Try to get all of your nails the same length (1/16 to 1/8 inch long). Then trim off hangnails and loose pieces of skin around your nails. Fingernails should be rounded and toenails should be cut straight across.

Step 2

File off any rough edges on your nails with an emery board.

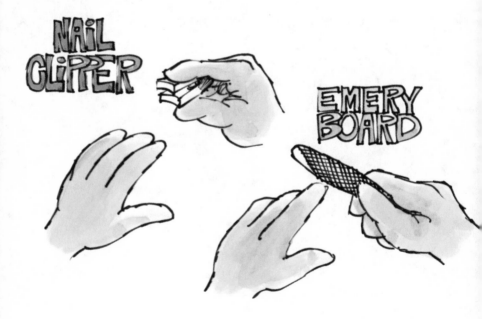

Step 3

Soak your hands and feet in warm soapy water for about ten minutes.

Step 4

Scrub under and on top of your nails with a manicure brush.

Step 5

Use a small cotton swab to clean the dirt around and under the fingernail that the brush can't get.

Step 6

Rinse your hands and feet in plain water.

Step 7

Use a clean dry towel to dry your hands and feet. As you are drying them, gently push back the cuticle on each finger and toe with the towel.

Please don't forget: even when you just wash your hands before a meal, use soap and rinse with water before drying your hands. To rinse your hands without soap puts some of the dirt on the towel and leaves the rest on your hands.

Step 8

Massage your hands and feet with lotion, working the lotion around and under your nails.

Avoid letting your nails get too long, because long nails hold more dirt and can get in the way when you are working and playing. Also avoid using nail polish, because it keeps your nails from "breathing" and growing properly.

THE END of the dirt on our bodies that bothers everyone!